Stems

By

Steffi Cavell-Clarke

©2017
Book Life
King's Lynn
Norfolk PE30 4LS

ISBN: 978-1-78637-151-5

Written by:
Steffi Cavell-Clarke

Edited by:
Charlie Ogden

Designed by:
Danielle Jones

A catalogue record for this book
is available from the British Library

PHOTO CREDITS

Stems

CONTENTS

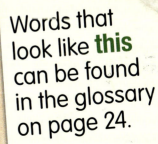

Words that look like **this** can be found in the glossary on page 24.

What Is a Plant?

A plant is a living thing. All living things need water, air and **sunlight** to live.

There are many different kinds of plant. Most plants have roots, leaves, flowers and a stem.

Plants live all around the world!

5

What Is a **Stem?**

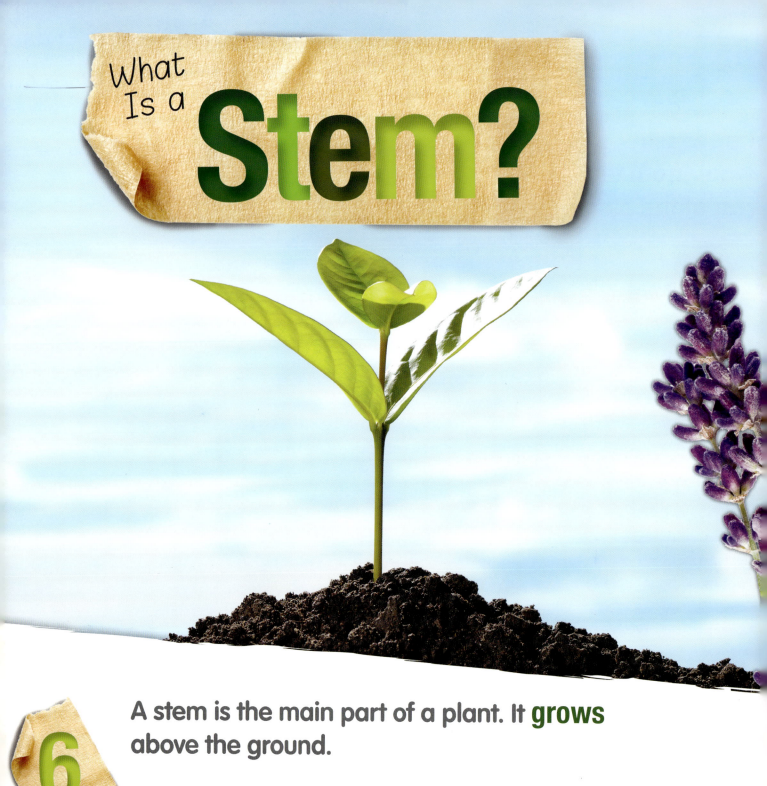

A stem is the main part of a plant. It **grows** above the ground.

6

The stem has many important jobs to do. It holds up the plant and carries water from the roots to the rest of the plant.

What Do **Stems** Look Like?

Tulip Stem

Cactus Stem

Bamboo Stem

Stems come in many different shapes and sizes.

A tree is a very large plant. It has a large stem, called a trunk, that is covered in a layer of bark. The bark helps to **protect** the tree.

Tree Trunk

9

How Do **Stems** Grow?

Out of a seed grows a tiny shoot. The shoot grows up through the soil and towards the sunlight.

10

The shoot grows into a stem and continues to grow above the soil. Later, leaves and flowers will grow from the stem.

→ must add water

Carrot

11

In order for the stem to grow, the plant needs water and sunlight. The plant's roots **absorb** water from the soil and then the water moves up into the stem.

The plant's leaves absorb sunlight, which gives the stem **energy** to grow.

13

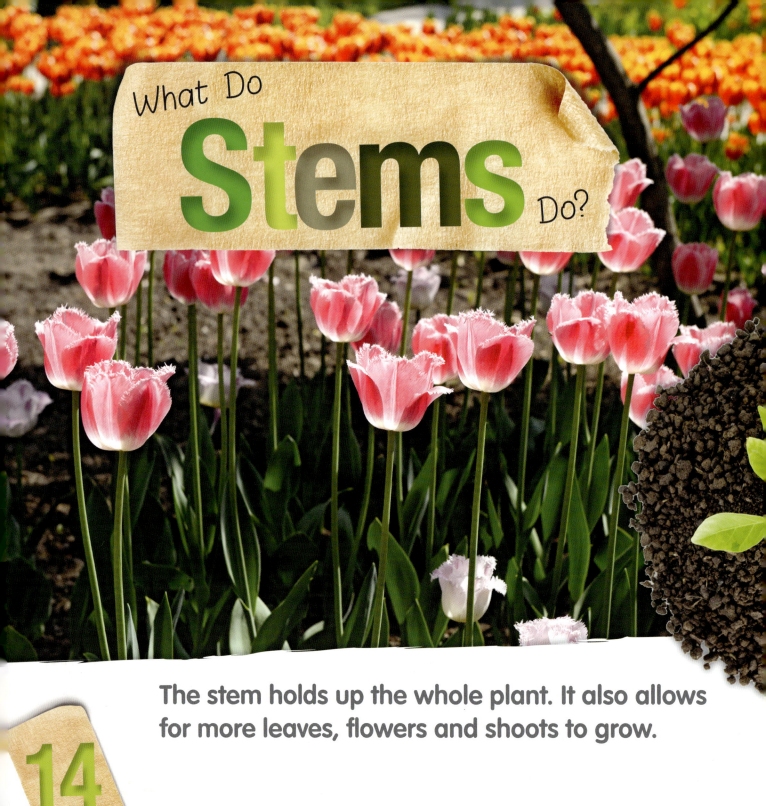

What Do Stems Do?

The stem holds up the whole plant. It also allows for more leaves, flowers and shoots to grow.

Stems usually grow straight and tall so that the plant's leaves are held up towards the sun. This helps the leaves to absorb sunlight so that they can make food for the plant.

Stems are filled with tiny tubes. These tubes are used to carry water from the roots to the other parts of the plant.

16

Food that is made in the leaves is carried through these tubes to other parts of the plant.

17

Strange Stems

Thorn

Rose

Some plants grow thorns or spines on their stems. This helps to protect the plant against animals that might try to eat it.

18

Plants that live in the **desert** are used to only having a small amount of water. Cactus plants have thick stems that store lots of water for the plant.

This cactus stores water in its thick stem.

19

Stems in the Forest

Branches

Trunk

Leaves

Forests are full of trees that have strong, thick trunks. Trees have strong trunks so that they can hold up lots of branches and leaves.

The tallest trees in the world are redwood trees. Their trunks can grow to be over 100 metres tall.

Redwood Tree

These giant trees can live to be 2,000 years old!

21

Tasty Stems

Broccoli

Celery

Rhubarb

Watch out! Rhubarb leaves are **poisonous**.

There are some stems that are safe for humans to eat, such as celery, rhubarb and broccoli.

Many animals eat stems too. Giant pandas love to eat bamboo stems and leaves!

Giant Panda

Bamboo

23

GLOSSARY

absorb soak up

desert an area of land that receives very little rain

energy the power needed to do something

forests areas of land covered in trees

grows naturally develops and increases in size

poisonous dangerous or deadly when eaten

protect look after and keep safe

sunlight light from the sun

INDEX